JOURNEY INTO *Blindness*

*An Inspirational Story of Overcoming Trauma
and Regaining a Valuable Life*

KENT CHRISTY

JOURNEY INTO BLINDNESS
AN INSPIRATIONAL STORY OF OVERCOMING
TRAUMA AND REGAINING A VALUABLE LIFE

iUniverse books may be ordered through booksellers or by contacting:

iUniverse
1663 Liberty Drive
Bloomington, IN 47403
www.iuniverse.com
1-800-Authors (1-800-288-4677)

Because of the dynamic nature of the Internet, any web addresses or links contained in this book may have changed since publication and may no longer be valid. The views expressed in this work are solely those of the author and do not necessarily reflect the views of the publisher, and the publisher hereby disclaims any responsibility for them.

Any people depicted in stock imagery provided by Thinkstock are models, and such images are being used for illustrative purposes only. Certain stock imagery © Thinkstock.

ISBN: 978-1-5320-2829-8 (sc)
ISBN: 978-1-5320-2830-4 (e)

Library of Congress Control Number: 2017911151

Print information available on the last page.

iUniverse rev. date: 07/17/2017

CONTENTS

PREFACE

As I was emerging from depression and into a state of acceptance of the loss of my eyesight, I got a whim to write a book about my experience. My wife, Alexis, challenged me to write this book.

I worked with coach and mentor Melanie from Inspiring Women to Regain Energy, who encouraged me and provided the emotional motivation factor. She helped me define the road map and identify what I wanted to write and what steps were needed to accomplish the work. Because of Melanie's help, it was clear in my mind why I needed to write the book for my own emotional healing and how it could be inspirational to others experiencing loss. I appreciate what my new friend Melanie has done for me.

A special thank-you goes out to my wife, Alexis, for all her secretarial work in keying in my words, doing the needed research for specific sections, and editing the manuscript. The process of working through the emotional turmoil of my loss while writing this book has increased the bond between us.

And last but not least, special appreciation goes to my family and friends who have critiqued my work and given input for my book. Since I was not a literary giant, I needed help and structure. Many thanks go to Mary from Mary Groll Marketing; Ellen from the Bucks County Association for the Blind and Visually Impaired; Jeanne, author of *Between Now and Then*; my thoughtful neighbors John and Donna; and my dear friend Chad. These caring folks have put extensive time and energy into editing the manuscript. Bruce from Bruce P. Kinsey Photography took my visual idea and made it into a spectacular silhouette of my journey. Kay from Brand New World Marketing developed a creative website and video for my book.

INTRODUCTION

I WROTE THIS book to help others understand what it is like to go blind or to lose a large portion of your well-being through some type of life-changing disability. Going totally blind, in many ways, is probably not so different from the experience of losing a limb, developing a debilitating illness, or going through the trauma of losing a loved one or even a home. My hope is that the description of my journey will be helpful to those experiencing blindness or any other type of loss and be an interesting story for all.

Through the communication of my experiences, I am testifying to others that it is possible to work through the many ups and downs of a challenging journey. It is possible to move forward and get back to the business of living your life. In addition, family, friends, and caregivers can gain insight and understanding into the process of loss and thereby provide better informed support.

Chapter 1

STAGES OF GRIEF

A s INDIVIDUALS, WE all suffer in different ways as we go through the stages of grief due to some loss. It's easy to lose hope and feel that we cannot go on after whatever we have experienced. But we have to go through a myriad of experiences in each of these stages before we are ready to move forward and play the hand of cards dealt to us.

I include the stages of grief in this work because, in my personal journey, I have experienced and worked through each. The order in which these stages occur can vary, and the time spent in each stage can differ as well. We can leave a stage and return back to it at a later time. Hopefully in the process, we rebuild our lives and find acceptance and hope.

Kübler-Ross Model: Five Stages of Grief

The Swiss doctor Elizabeth Kübler-Ross, MD, introduced the stages of grief in her 1969 book *On Death and Dying*. She had been studying the emotional state of severely ill people. The model Kübler-Ross developed applies to anyone facing past or impending loss, whether it be sight, a limb, a home, a friend or loved one, or even your own impending death. The following information of this grief model is from her book:

- **Denial and Isolation:** "The first reaction may be a state of shock" followed by denial (Kübler 1969, 40). A typical response might be "No, not me, it cannot be true" (Kübler 1969, 37).
- **Anger:** "When the first stage of denial cannot be maintained any longer, it is replaced by feelings of anger, rage, envy, and resentment ... [A response in this

phase might be:] 'Why me?'" (Kübler 1969, 49).

- **Bargaining:** In the bargaining stage, the individual hopes that the cause of grief can be avoided through negotiations or "some sort of an agreement which may postpone the inevitable happening" (Kübler 1969, 79).

- **Depression:** When the bargaining fails to achieve the desired result, "a sense of great loss" or depression can follow (Kübler 1969, 83).

- **Acceptance:** With "enough time ... and help in working through the previously described stages, he will reach a stage during which he is neither depressed nor angry about his fate ... Acceptance should not be mistaken for a happy stage," just an acceptance or embracing of the reality and a more stable condition of emotions (Kübler 1969, 109-110).

Kübler-Ross goes on to say,

> We have discussed ... the different stages that people go through when faced with tragic news, defense mechanisms in psychiatric terms, coping mechanisms to deal with extremely difficult situations. These means will last for different periods of time and will replace each other or exist at times side by side. The one thing that usually persists through all these stages is hope. (Kübler 1969, 133–134)

Journey into Blindness describes my experience of what it was like to become blind in a relatively short period of time and relate my emotional ups and downs to the Kübler-Ross model. I now have progressed and accepted my disability. However, sometimes I slip back to a stage I wish I had fully passed. I work my way through the emotions and then keep moving forward.

Chapter 2

HISTORY OF A MAN

M ANY PEOPLE HAVE asked me, "What happened to your eyes?" This chapter is intended to answer part of this question and provide insight into experiences that shaped my personality and gave me the ability to cope with the ups and downs of a challenging journey.

In 1948, when President Harry Truman was in office and I was eighteen months old, my mother, Agnes, saw an intermittent anomaly that looked like a red sparkle in my right eye. Aunt Helen also spotted it. The red sparkle would disappear, and then sometimes it would return. I think the visibility of the red sparkle was related to the way in which the sunlight reflected in my right eye.

5

Fortunately my mom did not take any chances. She took me to the family doctor, who referred me to Dr. Capriati, an ophthalmologist in Souderton, Pennsylvania. When Dr. Capriati looked at my right eye, he felt something was really wrong and referred me to Wills Eye Hospital in Philadelphia.

When we arrived in Philadelphia, a hospital ophthalmologist did more testing and determined that a tumor was present on the optic nerve behind my right eye. At that point, I was admitted to the hospital and readied for surgery.

Kent in 1948 before surgery.

In 1948, technology was not as advanced as it is today, and no highly focused radiation to the tumor and surrounding tissue was available. Following the removal of my right eye, tumor, and optic nerve, "radioactive seeds" were placed inside my eye cavity to provide continual radiation and ensure that any remaining malignancy would be destroyed. The doctors at Wills Eye constructed a backing or spherical implant in my right eye socket so that a prosthetic could be used to resemble the good left eye.

As a toddler, I got through the surgery well. One day when my mom came to visit me at the hospital, she found me in a crib with a restricting overhead grate. It seems as though I was bouncing up and down having fun and I bounced right out of the crib. The nurses thought I needed to be contained and put a safety cover over the crib.

When Mom wanted to go home, she would say, "Goodbye, Kent."

I responded with "bye" and continued playing with the interesting and exciting hospital toys.

Mom felt a bit hurt because I did not seem to care if she left me there. Since I had an infant brother at home, I was accustomed to Mom's attention elsewhere. I was confident she would be back for me.

Before I started school, an acrylic prosthetic was made for my right eye socket, painted to resemble the good left eye. The prosthetic is not a glass sphere or eyeball. It is a curved portion of the surface of a sphere, a curved polygon. The prosthetic fits in my eye socket and rests up against the implanted sphere. This prosthetic looked like my real left eye, but movement of my right eye was not well coordinated with the left.

At night, my mom would clean the prosthetic and set it in a glass in the bathroom to soak overnight in a borax solution. I thought it a good idea to have an eye looking up at my mom and dad at night when they washed their faces before bed.

As I grew up, I only looked through my left eye and thought this was normal. Certainly it was the normal for me. I had no binocular vision, thus no depth perception, and did not understand what I was missing. I just knew I was different from other children.

By first grade, other children could see that my two eyes did not always move exactly together.

Sometimes kids would look at me queerly and ask, "What is wrong with your eye?" The questions were not continuous, just every so often when I was playing or walking down a hallway. These questions made me feel uncomfortable because I didn't know how to respond. As a result, I became self-conscious and rather shy. If my mother had gone to my first-grade teacher and asked someone to explain to the class that I had only one eye and why, it would have been a great deal easier emotionally for me because my classmates would have understood why I looked different.

By third grade, most of my classmates were familiar with my situation, accepted me as I was, and became my good friends. We had been together for more than two years and played together as a group. I had gained confidence and came out of my shell. If someone remarked or asked a question, it didn't matter anymore.

By fifth grade, I was old enough to remove and replace the prosthetic. One day, when tired of being teased by a classmate, I took the prosthetic out of the right eye socket and chased a girl with it. My mom scolded me for this.

My response to my mom was "That girl won't bother me anymore."

Kent in elementary school. The prosthetic matched the good left eye in this photo.

By eighth grade, I could relate and interact with the guys but not the girls. I could not look girls directly into their eyes because I felt self-conscious about my prosthetic. Like lots of teens, I lacked self-confidence and felt awkward.

Here's an interesting thought: In my mom's Pennsylvania Dutch culture, when I was ten or twelve, my mother told me, "If you play with yourself, you will go blind." It took only fifty years for this to happen. Well, some say Mom was right.

I liked playing sports and had an innate athletic ability. However, I was not good at ball sports because of my lack of binocular vision and depth perception. To understand exactly where the ball was going and how fast it would get there required the depth perception of two coordinated eyes. In baseball, coaches usually put me in the outfield. Since I could not judge where the ball was going, I would not put myself in the correct position to catch it. Sometimes I would wind up getting hit by the ball. As I got older, "at bat" or "catching in the field" was not as difficult because, even though I could not "triangulate" using two eyes, I was able to understand the size and speed of the ball as a result of my experience. Once I knew the type and size of something, I could judge its distance and speed and compensate for my lack of depth perception.

My wife has always said, "Throw something to Kent, and he will probably drop it the first time. Throw it a second time, and he might catch it or might not. But by the third time, he always catches the object and will never miss thereafter."

When growing up, one of my favorite baseball players was Ted Williams, number nine of the Boston Red Sox, because he was a left fielder with a perfect swing and 521 lifetime home runs (Redsox.com 2017). I liked Stan Musial, number six of the St. Louis Cardinals, who played as an outfielder and first baseman. Stan Musial had 3,630 National League hits and 475 home runs (Cardinals.com 2017). Richie Ashburn, number six of the Philadelphia Phillies, was another favorite because, once on base, he would usually score a run. Richie Ashburn was able to achieve

1,114 runs in his baseball career (Malcolm 2009). And of course Hank Aaron of the Atlanta Braves was another favorite. Hank was mostly a right fielder and currently holds the second-highest home run record of 755 runs (Braves.com 2017).

My dad encouraged me to take up golf. He would take me around to his friends and cronies to show off my drive. One of my dad's friends kindly took me aside and told me not to swing a golf club like a baseball bat. Instead, think of swinging flat around the face of a clock to prevent slices and hooks. Overall I was pretty good at golf, particularly my drive down the fairways. However, without depth perception, judging the distance to the green and choosing the correct club to use often left the ball short of the green or beyond it.

Many years later, after not playing golf for twenty years, I was invited to play in an AC Delco golf tournament associated with a Dover NASCAR race. In this tournament, I won the long drive contest because I had power and remembered the advice from my dad's friend. But my score was nothing to brag about because my iron play was horrendous due to no depth perception and the lack of recent experience on a course.

Graduation from North Penn High School in 1964. The right eye prosthetic is not teaming well in this photo.

When I turned sixteen and got a driver's license, I had no problem driving because, knowing the size of cars, I could understand how far away they were. I could maintain an appropriate distance from the vehicle in front of me. The only difficulty was backing up because I could not easily judge the distance between the back of my car and the objects I was backing up to.

I always wanted to race cars, but with only one eye and no depth perception, I would not feel comfortable in a pack of racing cars, especially with no vision on my right side.

I was able to comfortably enjoy competitive racing in go-karts because of their smaller size and three-quarter-inch proximity to the ground. I could hear the sound of a go-kart engine coming up on my right side, the side with no eye. I did have peripheral vision on my left side; thus I could see someone approaching on my left.

I ran a competitive go-kart in the 100cc Yamaha Pipe Heavy class. In fact, one year I won third-place point championship at Great Meadows in Hacketstown, New Jersey.

Several years later, I won the third-place point championship two years in a row at Oakland Valley Race Park near Port Jervis, New York.

I enjoyed wrenching or working on my own kart. At an event, the day consisted of warm-ups and three heats or races per class, ending with a trophy in each class for persons accumulating the highest number of points. During warm-ups, I sometimes needed to change out gears to improve lap time. Between warm-ups and before each heat, I checked tire pressure, oiled the kart chain, changed clutch oil, and sometimes changed out the tires. Because of the high revolutions per minute and small amount of oil in the clutch, I would engage the clutch at 9,800 revolutions per minute, and the engine would rev up to 14,000 revolutions per minute on a straightaway. With proper gear ratio, I could run the kart sixty to sixty-five miles per hour on a long straightaway. The responsiveness and maneuverability of the kart in corners brought out my skill. The entire experience was so exhilarating. I loved go-karting and the challenge of intense competition.

Kent competitively racing his go-
kart around the track.

Kent posing with checkered
flag behind his go-kart.

I sold auto parts for my entire working life, mostly for the same employer. I loved dealing with my customers. I enjoyed developing relationships and prided myself on staying up with technical knowledge. I liked what I did. As a "motor head," I thrived on the auto parts business. I enjoyed interacting with my customers, getting technical information for them, and solving their parts problems. I was keenly interested in how brakes, motors, and transmissions worked and how all the systems fit together. I loved cars and auto parts so much that I used my skills and did most of my own car repairs.

Let me backtrack a bit. I had two brothers: Billy, who was one year younger than I was, and Charles, who was ten years older. Charles bought me my first bicycle and taught me an appreciation for the outdoors through fishing and small game hunting. Even today, Charles calls me often just to talk and make sure I am doing well. I appreciate all that Charles has done for me, and I am so thankful for him.

Billy and I were extremely close and did

everything together. One fall day when Billy was fourteen years old, he came home from school feeling discouraged because he had trouble running in gym. It turns out that Billy had leukemia, and on Christmas Eve, he died of this disease. I was numb. I lost my brother and closest friend that day.

From that point on, Christmas was a downer. I was angry but could not deal with the emotion of this loss. A big part of my life was taken away. In denial, my defense mechanism totally blocked out experiences with him. From that point on, I was always sad Christmas Eve and Christmas Day.

One year when I was in my midforties, my wife made a beautiful red velour Santa costume for me, and I bought a white beard and wig. At first, I was reluctant to play Santa, but once I witnessed children's reactions, being Santa was spectacular. It was the closest thing to being a god. So for fifteen years, I was Santa at Christmastime, and I would get into lengthy discussions with the kids. This was really fun for me.

Picture this. One year, three, large Colmar, Pennsylvania, fire engines were screaming north on Route 309. With piercing sirens and bright red lights flashing, I was on top of the lead engine. The fire engines delivered Santa to a company brunch. Thirty excited children sat on my lap that day. What a fantastic time!

My wife reminds me that when Santa went to a back room to change into street clothes, he had no trousers. Santa forgot his pants at the fire station. So I traveled around in my Santa costume until my wife found a fireman to open the fire house door to retrieve my pants.

When no children were around, I was a risqué Santa with the ladies. They would sit on my lap as I made lewd suggestions about Christmas gifts. One year at a party, I even did a Santa strip tease. I had everyone laughing.

For fifteen years, being Santa kept me from sadness and depression at Christmastime. It helped me work though the loss of my brother. Now I can no longer be Santa for the children, because a blind Santa just does not fit into the wonder of Christmas. I miss the fun and awe of the children sitting on my lap and telling me their wishes.

Even though I can no longer be Santa around children, I still enjoy the excitement of the holiday season. In fact, recently I was able to be a blind Santa at a luncheon for the Bucks County Association for the Blind and Visually Impaired and had an enjoyable time. I can still hand out candy canes and crack jokes to help everyone have fun. My "Ho, ho, ho" is still alive!

Chapter 3

JOURNEY INTO BLINDNESS

I LIVED THROUGH my childhood and most of my adult life with only one eye. I coped extremely well until age sixty-three when my good eye began to fail. This chapter describes the happenings that left me with zero vision.

In the autumn of 2009, as I approached my sixty-third birthday, I began having problems with my left eye, my only eye. I could not keep my eyelid up without using tape. I tolerated this eyelid droop problem using tape for almost a year and then began to notice that my eye movement was hampered. When driving and changing lanes, I had to turn my whole body to the right to see cars or things on the right and to see whether it was safe or not to make a lane change. Shortly thereafter, I was having a problem with light. My eye remained dilated, which meant I could not see clearly in bright light. It was like trying to see on a snowy slope on a bright, sunny day.

I began to put all the symptoms together and acknowledge that I had a problem. My eyelid did not work properly and was half-closed. My eye movement was restricted, so I needed to move my whole body to view around to my right side. And I could not focus properly in bright light.

In August 2010, at age sixty-four, I went to an optometrist in Sellersville, Pennsylvania. After an eye examination, he told me that my problem was related to allergies. This did not make sense, yet I did not motivate myself to pursue another opinion. What a terrible mistake.

Six months later in February 2011, I had an examination by an ophthalmologist who insisted on an MRI and a CT scan. Based on the findings, I was referred to another ophthalmologist, an eye socket specialist at Wills Eye Hospital in Philadelphia. He ordered a second set of MRIs and CT scans, which confirmed a meningioma tumor putting pressure on my third cranial nerve. This nerve is responsible for eyelid movement; eye movement up, down, and toward the nose; the focusing of the eye lens; and the dilation of the pupil. Interestingly the sixth cranial nerve moves the eye away from the nose, and I did not lose this ability.

I was then referred to a neurosurgeon at Thomas Jefferson Hospital in Philadelphia. At the end of March 2011, he scheduled a biopsy of the parasellar mass, which confirmed a nonmalignant meningioma tumor of arachnoid cells. Consequently the biopsy also limited my sense of smell and damaged some of my taste buds. The left side of my palate at the top of my mouth became sensitive to touch and would get a tingling feeling. Food just did not taste the same. Eventually most of the sense of smell and taste did return. However, my sense of smell is not as keen as it once had been.

The meninges is a thin membrane covering the brain and spinal cord. It is composed of three layers: dura mater, arachnoid, and pia mater. It appears that arachnoid cells migrated outside my meninges and colonized in various locations on its surface, in other words, on the outside of my brain.

The neurosurgeon described this tumor as rubbery and sticky and growing in many locations. It was very slow-growing and difficult to remove. My tumor may have been a consequence of the radioactive seeds following the surgery in 1948 since large doses of radiation to the head may be a risk factor for meningioma tumors.

The American Brain Tumor Association reports information about meningioma tumors on their website,

> Between 40% and 80% of meningiomas contain an abnormal chromosome 22. The cause of this abnormality is not known. We do know, however, that this chromosome is normally involved in suppressing tumor growth. Meningiomas also frequently have extra copies of the platelet-derived growth factor (PDGFR) and epidermal growth factor receptors (EGFR), which

may contribute to the growth of these tumors.

Previous radiation to the head, a history of breast cancer, or neurofibromatosis type2 [Recklinghausen's disease] may be risk factors for developing meningioma. Multiple meningiomas occur in 5% to 15% of patients, particularly those with neurofibromatosis type 2.

Some meningiomas have receptors that interact with hormones, including progesterone, androgen, and less commonly, estrogen. Although the exact role of hormones in the growth of meningiomas has not been determined, researchers have observed that meningiomas occasionally grow faster during pregnancy. (American Brain Tumor Association 2014)

Meningioma tumors often go undetected. A problem occurs when the tumor grows into something like cranial nerves, the optic nerve, or blood vessels to the brain. That's when you experience symptoms, realize you have a problem, and seek a medical diagnosis and treatment.

Since radiation was prescribed, a radiologist at Lehigh Valley Hospital in Allentown, Pennsylvania, evaluated me in April 2011. Allentown was much easier for me to get to than Philadelphia. Fractionated stereotactic radiation was prescribed to deter additional growth of the meningioma. This treatment would not destroy the tumor. It would just stop or stunt its growth. I was told that the radiation could damage my optic nerve, causing loss of sight. The doctors said that my sight would "probably return." Was "probably" good enough to pursue the radiation treatment? I did not consider "sight probably would return" good enough, so I went on my way, working at my job in auto parts sales.

Eighteen months later, by October 2012, my sight deteriorated to the point where I could no longer drive. One rainy night, I did not notice soon enough that a car making a left-hand turn was stopped in front of me. I jammed on my brakes but still bumped into the back of the car.

The car then turned left, and I turned left as well. I stopped. The car I bumped continued on. Sure do wonder why that car did not stop. Needless to say, I sadly turned in my keys.

After I gave up driving, I began walking the mile and a half to work each day. As the vision in my eye deteriorated further, it got to a point where I could no longer recognize denominations of money. Even with a magnifying glass, I could not read the parts catalogs or computer screen. This made my job impossible. I sometimes had to get a colleague to read the parts catalog to me.

To complicate things further, I had a cataract in my left eye, my only eye. I sought cataract surgery in November 2012, hoping to improve my vision. After the cataract surgery, my vision became worse because the cataract was not the only problem with my vision. I wanted to continue working, but I could no longer read the paper and computer catalogs, even with a magnifying glass. Any hardware and software systems available to read the computer screen were too time-consuming for me to service my busy customers. I could no longer work. I could see shapes and people, but nothing was clear. I tried to do some chores around the house, and I continued to cook breakfast and dinner for my wife.

I felt discouraged. I had worked all my life and now was unable to do so. I wasn't ready to retire. I wanted to work at least five more years. I was only sixty-six and had lots more energy. Work had allowed me to have money to pay bills and enjoy leisure time. When I was working, I enjoyed my relationships with colleagues and customers, and I felt I was accomplishing something of value. I had been competent in my job, which I could no longer do. Wow, what a letdown. All this occurred in just three years' time.

I tried everything I could think of to regain my vision. In addition to seeking advice from excellent doctors at world-renowned Wills Eye Hospital and Thomas Jefferson Hospital, I tried Syntonics colored light therapy, nutrition, acupuncture, and Chinese herbs in hopes of achieving improved vision. Nothing worked. That is, nothing worked to stop the tumor growth and restore my optic nerve. Nutritionals gave me more energy, and acupuncture helped with improved sleep, but my vision kept getting worse because the tumor continued to grow and put pressure on my optic nerve.

My sight continued to deteriorate. By the end of January 2013, I agreed to meningioma surgery at Thomas Jefferson Hospital. The surgery was necessary to clean out some of the meningioma cells that were encroaching on my optic nerve. I hoped the optic nerve would recover.

In early February 2013, my surgeons made a twelve-inch incision from the middle of my left ear, along my hairline up the side of my skull, and across the top of my forehead directly above the middle of my right eye socket. The surgeons then pulled back my skin to expose the bone. They cut a rectangular section out of my skull and then gently moved my brain aside to get to the area of the meningioma.

Scraping away the tumor was difficult. According to one doctor, it was rubbery and sticky. After getting as much of the tumor as possible, the doctors gently moved my brain back in place and inserted a titanium plate over the bone opening. Titanium screws still hold this plate in place today. The incision was closed up with sutures. The entire surgery took five and a half hours and went as well as possible. Now I have my own permanently implanted hard hat. I thank all the doctors and staff for their excellent care.

Oh, by the way, one surgeon told me that several bats flew out when he opened up my skull. I've always heard the metaphor "bats in the belfry," but never thought it would apply to me.

In preparing me for the surgery, my wife cut my hair to a half-inch length so one side would not be four inches long and the other side shaved during surgery. Actually everyone said I looked younger with short hair; thus I keep the short hairstyle today. Another thing my wife did was shave my forearms. The nurses said this was a great idea because they did not need to rip hair when taking off the tape from all the needles, medical drips, monitors, and so forth.

I do recommend to everyone shaving forearms before surgery.

Following the surgery in February, I felt hopeful that my optic nerve would start to regenerate and reverse the neuropathy of the optic nerve. I could see images but had lost the ability to see color. It was as if I were sitting in a dim room with a minimal amount of light and just barely recognizing shapes and forms. I could still walk the two miles to the Towne Restaurant in Telford for a soup and sandwich lunch. I could do some chores around the house, and I continued to cook on an electric stove. I still cook today.

My eyesight continued to deteriorate. Six months after the meningioma surgery in the fall of 2013, I had zero vision. You could flash and blink a light directly into my eye, and I could not tell if it were on or off. I now had lost 80 percent of my life and my independence. From the time I began to incur vision problems to the time of total darkness, just four years had passed.

At this point, the prosthetic in my right eye no longer fit properly, so I used a black patch on my right eye. When children looked concerned or frightened, my wife would say, "Oh, don't mind him. He thinks he's a pirate." This humorous intervention would help the children relax and no longer feel afraid.

I do not know if my life would improve if I had a service dog. I applied to The Seeing Eye in Morristown, New Jersey, for one. I understood I would need to train at The Seeing Eye location for a month to get acquainted with the dog and learn how to use this service. I had recommendations from my doctor, my mobility trainer at the Bureau of Blindness and Visual Services, my chiropractor, and a friend.

All suggested a service dog would be a wonderful aid for me. Someone from The Seeing Eye came to my home, and we walked together outside. This person gave me the impression that all seemed okay and I could train with the dog.

However, a week later, a response came from The Seeing Eye in Morristown, "Since you do not have a job or volunteer position in which to use the dog, you do not qualify. You do not have a regular destination."

I was shocked that my request had been denied. I am not sure the real reason for the denial, but since I am getting along quite fine right now, I will not further pursue getting a service dog.

Chapter 4

A BAD DAY

A BAD DAY: I thought I slept okay, but when I went downstairs, I made some stupid mistakes. I had become upset because my wife was unhappy at an error she had made. My wife has an incredible workload. She has her responsibilities and then tries to do what I cannot. I once did so many things easily. Now I either struggle to accomplish a task or simply cannot do it at all. I feel inadequate. Believing I put more burden on my wife makes me feel even morc inadequate and terrible.

While making breakfast this day, I dropped a knife and could not find it. Then after placing a pan on the stove, I just could not align it correctly on the burner. Cooking the eggs was okay, but when I tried to fold over the omelet, it was difficult for me to get a feel using the silicone flipper, and I spilled some of the eggs outside the pan. I lost my orientation and then bumped into things—the wall with my head, a cabinet with my knee, and a table leg with my foot.

All these small things accumulated, and I became very frustrated and upset. I can't seem to shed the little things. Then I fall apart, and everything gets messed up. I feel sorry for myself and cannot deal with anything. My voice becomes faint. I even get tears in my eyes. I get so depressed.

I resent the fact that I am blind. Things I once did so easily have become almost impossible. I can't do what I want to do and can't appreciate the things I once loved. I guess it boils down to the fact that, at times, particularly when little things accumulate, I feel sorry for myself. Then I have a hard time recovering.

After a period of time of feeling angry, frustrated, and sorry for myself and questioning "Why me?" I come back to my normal attitude.

I don't have clinical depression. It's just a downtime of feeling sorry for myself. It passes, and then I am back to my normal self.

Overload: My wife recently took me for a relaxing weekend to Atlantic City, New Jersey. We stayed at the Flagship, where we had been several times before. I enjoyed the food at the Blue Water Grille and used the hot tub in the building. However during this mini-vacation, I had difficulty orienting myself in the room. I often seemed to be going the wrong way to get to my destination, whether it was the kitchenette table, the refrigerator, or the bed.

When leaving the resort, my wife and I made several trips to get our luggage and cooler to the car. I often wanted to turn the wrong way. After leaving the resort, my wife drove to the Tropicana Casino for lunch and parked in the parking garage. We walked from the garage to the elevator, which took us to the casino complex. We walked through a shopping mall called the Quarter and then into the casino and the buffet area for lunch. There were many turns, elevators, and escalators, along with lots of loud whistles, bells, noise, and commotion. I became confused and felt a definite disconnect.

I think the confusion is a result of experiencing too much stimulation for my brain to process when I cannot see what is around me. Then when walking through the serving area of the buffet and trying to process what my wife was telling me, I became totally frustrated. Overwhelmed, I got upset and could not deal with the situation. I could not even make a decision as to an omelet or sunny-side eggs. Fortunately a compassionate chef understood my frustration and heard a bit of what I was saying. He prepared a plate for me of sunny-side eggs, potatoes, and bacon. My wife guided me back to the table to sit down. Wow, what a frustrating and disorienting experience. At the table, I was finally able to catch my breath, calm down, and get a perspective as to what was happening around me.

My wife and I discussed what had just occurred. I think I will be much better prepared to go into these hectic and confusing situations in the future. I should have recognized that I was becoming overwhelmed and mentioned that I needed to sit down to unwind. My wife now knows to look for signs of overload and help me take a timely break.

A Bad Night: Every so often, I sleep only two to three hours a night and then wake up with nervous energy and too many thoughts. I cannot settle my mind and get back to sleep. I have to get up and move around before going back to bed. In the morning, I get up to help my wife get off to work, and then I go back to bed to sleep for a couple more hours. This gets me into an abnormal cycle where I might not sleep properly for days or weeks. With an inadequate night's sleep, I am not functional and sharp-thinking during the day. When I get into these abnormal sleep cycles, I become very moody.

The circadian rhythm sleep disorder, also known as Non-24, is a condition experienced by some people who are blind. Our body clock gets out of sync, probably because we cannot see the light difference between night and day, resulting in a shifting of our sleep cycle.

Motion Sickness: According to the Vision Therapy Center website,

> Functional vision problems are a big contributor to motion sickness ... A person's visual, auditory and vestibular system must be working in concert to give a person the information he or she needs to know where they are in space. Vision leads this integration of information, and when someone has vision problems, the visual information is not as complete as it could be. This leads to the feeling of being off balance or "motion sick." (Vision Therapy Center 2017)

I had never been a person to experience car sickness until I lost my sight. Now when riding in a car with many turns, starts, and stops, I occasionally experience motion sickness. Sometimes if I loosen my seat belt and breathe deep, the sickness lessens. Motion sickness has made long drives uncomfortable for me.

Chapter 5

EMOTIONAL UPS AND DOWNS

A FTER THE MENINGIOMA surgery in February 2013, I was really hoping that my optic nerve would regenerate itself. As time went on, realizing this was not happening, I started using the following positive affirmations:

- It is so nice that I can see the flowers.
- It is great that I can drive again.
- I am enjoying reading this interesting book.

After three weeks or so of affirmations, I tried breathing meditation and sometimes meditation with mantras to clear my mind and heal my optic nerve in hopes that I would see well again. However, with every week, my eyesight kept deteriorating because my optic nerve neuropathy increased.

I started a regime of prayer. I prayed to God that he would restore my vision. If He would restore my vision, I would start volunteering and do anything I could to help other people. It seems as though I was experiencing the bargaining stage of grief. Despite weeks of continuous prayer, my eyesight kept deteriorating to the point that I was totally blind and could not even see light.

After trying the affirmations, meditation, and prayer for many weeks, I realized I was totally blind. I became very angry. I kept asking, "Why me? What have I done to deserve this? I have only one eye. Why take sight from this one?"

My anger became so great that it prevented me from doing the things I was really capable of doing. I sat and sulked. The anger turned into more intense grief, and I continued feeling sorry for myself. I was not dealing well with the situation. All I kept thinking was, *This is just not right. This is so unfair and wrong. Why punish me?*

After the denial, anger, and bargaining of grief, depression followed. I was unable to sleep. I had no appetite and could not eat. I asked myself, *Do I really want to spend the rest of my life being totally blind?* At that point, I contemplated ways I could end my life without it looking like suicide. I spent hours and days thinking about how to do it. *Could I think myself into a terminal disease? Maybe I could initiate a heart attack, which would take me out quickly.*

The "taking my life" thoughts lasted about a month. The only thing that helped me dismiss them was my family and friends. I have always been rational, and I knew the guilt and grief I would inflict on my family and friends would be painful. I understood that taking my life would be a greedy, self-centered action, hurting the people who loved me. As a result, I eliminated all thoughts of suicide because it would hurt those I loved and eliminate all the joy, love, empathy, and positive relationships of life. Suicide became unacceptable.

In March 2013, my wife took me to a therapist whom I saw on a regular basis for seven months.

Sue was a compassionate social worker, in Doylestown, Pennsylvania. Eleven months later, I saw another social worker, Patty, at the Penn Foundation in Sellersville, Pennsylvania, for four months.

All these therapy sessions allowed me to open up and talk about things I was uncomfortable discussing with my wife or friends. The sessions helped me work through my frustration and the anger of not being able to do what I once did. The social workers coached me to discover a pathway to move on with my life. This helped me accept my blindness and understand that my life still had value.

I had been a person who seldom used four-letter words. Rarely would I let out a curse word and never the F-word. As I became more and more frustrated and depressed from my vision loss, nasty words became a frequent part of my vocabulary, especially if I bumped into something, dropped anything, or could not accomplish what I was trying to do. I've cleaned up my vocabulary considerably now and express these words only when I bang my head into something or hit my sore knee. I apologize to my two grandsons who heard my bad language.

All in all, it took me almost two years to face the fact that I was blind and would be for the rest of my life. No one could do this for me. I had to adjust my mind-set and understand this for myself. Now that I accept this fact, I can go on with my life. I can do what I am capable of doing and enjoy that I am alive. I can smell the flowers and appreciate the people who love and support me. Yes, I do revert back to feeling sorry for myself at times, but I quickly return to my new way of dealing with blindness. I affirm my will to live and to enjoy my life.

So what does a person with vision loss do with his or her time? The Carnegie Library in Pittsburgh supplies digital talking books and players to legally blind people free of charge. I now have read or listened to numerous books on a wide range of topics: classics, mysteries, adventure, science and technology, science fiction, biographies, sports, history, and other nonfiction. I receive several current periodicals on disk, which keep me up on current events.

The Library for the Blind and Physically Handicapped of the Free Library of Philadelphia supply the periodicals.

I love music, and I love to dance. Music helps me get back into a good mood. I listen to numerous music CDs in a wide range of styles. Music from different time periods helps invoke happy memories from the past. Talking books expand my knowledge and open up my mind to many new avenues of thought. Talking books and enjoyable CDs help to keep me out of depression and moving forward with the positive aspects of my life and not reverting back to the negatives.

I love people and enjoy talking with them. However, I get really frustrated when I am talking with someone who walks away without letting me know he or she is leaving the discussion. I continue to talk into the air and look very stupid. When I discover that I am talking to myself only, I get upset.

When at parties or group gatherings, people often set me safe in a chair. This isolates me because I am stuck in the chair and everyone is constantly in motion. I feel alienated because I cannot fully engage with what is happening. I feel a sense of disconnect especially when the group is talking about a picture or things going on that require visual sight.

Now when at parties, I ask, "Where is everybody hanging out?" Then I say, "That's where I want to be. I want to be with everyone else." Being in the middle of the action allows me to be myself and interject my typical humor. I want to be part of the group.

Losing my vision has made delegating a necessity, and this has always been difficult for me. When I had my eyesight, I was mechanically inclined and would tackle any project around the house. If I were not familiar with a project, I would do the research and learn. I built brick sidewalks, a fifty-foot dry creek bed for drainage, and an aesthetic, Cambridge block retaining wall to keep garden soil from eroding into the creek bed. I created the landscaping and maintained the grass and gardens. I put a hardwood floor in a bedroom, installed a tile floor in a sunroom, painted walls, built shelves, made bookcases, tackled plumbing and electrical repairs, and did most of the maintenance and repair on my cars. Now without eyesight, I find most of these projects are just not possible for me. I can't even do the grocery shopping without help.

I sometimes get angry and withdrawn when I need to ask others for help with tasks, knowing I once could do them myself. I feel guilty leaving so many tasks up to my wife to complete. She is overwhelmed, and this makes me feel sad.

Sometimes when I am feeling down, my wife reminds me, "You could have died at age two if it were not for an astute mom and doctor. You have had all these years to enjoy life. Be appreciative and thankful."

Chapter 6

LEARNING TO LIVE
WITH BLINDNESS

O NCE I ACCEPTED the fact that I was blind and
there are many things I *can* do, I learned
to live more comfortably with my disability.
My depression subsided, and I became a life
participant once again. As mentioned earlier,
I enjoy listening to musical CDs and digital
talking books and doing much of the cooking.
You will often find me working at simple chores
around the house and sometimes even doing
repairs.

One problem is that the CDs don't always get
back into their original cases, and I lose track of
portions of my collection. For example, Taylor
Swift's *Red* CD got put into the Adele *21* case,

and the Adele *21* CD wound up in a Little Feet case. Fortunately my close friend Chad helps me maintain my CD collection. I am thankful and appreciative for his gracious help.

Putting on a coordinated outfit can be an adventure. To help me out, my wife organizes my closet in a rainbow fashion. She puts white shirts to the right, then going left are the beige, yellow, orange, red, green, blue, navy, gray, and then black. Same concept applies to my slacks. Fortunately I pick out a coordinated outfit 85 percent of the time. Only occasionally does my wife send me back upstairs to change my outfit.

While I am talking about outfits, I must tell you about my stylish, cost-effective, wraparound, safety sunglasses. Since I have no vision, one eye missing, and an eyelid that always stays closed, dark, wraparound sunglasses are a must when out in public. You can purchase a variety of inexpensive safety sunglasses online. I get them at my local NAPA auto parts store, the store where I once worked. I buy SAS Safety, dark tint, wraparound safety glasses, part number 5330 or 5331.

Navigating alone in my neighborhood can be challenging. I live in a quiet development that has little traffic during the day. One morning at six o'clock, I decided to take a bit of trash to the tote, which was outside at the curb for pickup. I used my white cane and walked down the driveway toward the garbage can.

Just at that time, my wife looked out the window and saw a commotion in the street. There I was in the middle of the street with cars stopped in each direction.

One kind gentleman got out of his car and asked, "Hey, buddy, can I help you? Do you know you are in the middle of the street?"

I did not realize that I had walked down the driveway, across the sidewalk, and down the driveway apron into the street.

Our development has several roads with sidewalks and many cul-de-sacs without them. One Saturday morning, before I owned an iPhone with GPS, I went out for a walk. I walked down the driveway, turned right at the sidewalk in front of my house onto Spring House Lane, and then turned right again at an intersection with Village Green Lane. I crossed a small road and continued on.

When I got to the intersection with Country Side, I knew the handicapped ramp was angled diagonally into the intersection. I felt the curb with my white cane, thought I was properly oriented, and started to walk across the street. Somehow I did not walk a straight line on Village Green Lane, but instead walked diagonally through the intersection and up Country Side. From this point on, I could not figure out where I was. I walked for a bit and then got lost for twenty minutes in a cul-de-sac. I got extremely frustrated and called my wife. I just sat down on the curb and waited for her to find me. It took my wife quite some time to locate me because I could not tell her which of the many cul-de-sacs I was in.

On another occasion, I ventured out for a walk and thought I was doing fine trying to backtrack to go home. However, I could find no sidewalk. I asked myself, "Where am I?"

When my wife called me from work, I explained I was lost. She called neighbors and sent them out to look for me. The neighbors had a difficult time finding me because I could not tell them my location. It seems as though I walked back to my road, Spring House Lane, crossed the street, and walked right past my house. I walked to the end of our road and into a town house development with no sidewalks. Boy, was I lost and frustrated!

iPhone: One of my biggest assets is my Apple iPhone. My wife purchased the iPhone for me because I was losing my way in the neighborhood. The iPhone has a Global Positioning System application, known as GPS, that can tell me where I am and give me verbal instructions to get back home.

Once I started learning what the iPhone could do, I realized it was a marvelous tool for a blind person. I have had numerous applications installed with the help of Gaye at Bucks County Association for the Blind and Visually Impaired: Google, iTunes, YouTube, Podcasts, News, Contacts, Calendar, Clock, Money Reading, Be My Eyes, and more. Everything is configured for voice instruction and voice reply. I can instruct

Siri to read my text messages, create a text, read it back, and then send the text. Siri can call someone in my contact list and more.

Siri on an iPhone is a talking application that comes with the phone's operating system. I can configure the voice to be male or female, American, English, or Australian. Siri tells me the time of day, the date, and the temperature outside. It tells me how to spell a word, gets me the definition of words, gives the scores for professional sports games, and much more. When I ask a question, Siri tries to connect me with different websites that can answer the question and reads me the information on the website.

Siri can open up the GPS application to help me navigate. The GPS integrates with Maps and can be configured for driving directions or walking instructions. In Contacts, I added an entry "Home," defined as my street address. Thus, when I am out, I can ask Siri to "Take me home," and the voice gives me the directions to guide me to my house.

Siri has a sense of humor and keeps me

laughing. When I ask for the temperature outside, Siri might respond, "Brr, the temperature is twenty-five degrees." If Siri cannot answer my question, it has various responses: "That's interesting," "I'm not allowed to say that," "I'm sorry. I'll try harder," or "I did not know that."

Siri helps keep me in touch with the world and out of isolation. It also helps to keep me out of depression. My wife teases me by saying that when I get up every morning, I ask Siri, "What's Taylor Swift's itinerary for the day?"

Be My Eyes is an interesting and helpful iPhone app based on an idea from the Danish furniture craftsman Hans Jorgen Wilberg (Demmitt 2015). When I activate Be My Eyes, a volunteer at the other end of the phone line tells me what he or she sees via the camera of my iPhone. The volunteer can help me read a document or find something lost by scanning the iPhone camera around the room. The volunteer can read me the label on a can or carton and read me an expiration date. When outside, I can use my iPhone camera to show the volunteer landmarks and help me understand where I am at. Be My Eyes is available in several countries and in different languages. I have used Be My Eyes when my wife was not home to help me.

The National Library Service for the Blind and Physically Handicapped (NLS), part of the Library of Congress, "administers a free library program of braille and audio materials circulated to eligible borrowers in the United States by postage-free mail." The Braille and Audio Reading Download (BARD) mobile application allows me to download any book in the Library of Congress. This program can also read the book to me, and I have enjoyed many books this way. I understand that the NLS also provides "braille, large-print, and recorded instructional materials about music and musicians" (NLS Factsheets 2015).

According to the NLS website, the

> NLS has partnered with the Bureau of Engraving and Printing (BEP) in support of its U.S. Currency Reader Program, which provides currency-reader devices, free of charge, to individuals who are blind or visually

impaired. The program is part of the government's Meaningful Access Initiative to assist individuals who experience difficulties identifying U.S. currency. The currency reader, called the iBill Talking Banknote Identifier, is a compact device that announces a note's value by voice, pattern of tones, or pattern of vibrations. Users insert a bill into the device and press the button on the device's side to have the denomination identified. (NLS: That All May Read 1975)

I have not used Apple AirPods cordless Bluetooth earbuds with access to Siri, optical character readers or note-taking software. I have not installed Adobe Digital Editions or Job Access with Speech (JAWS) Screen Reader on my computer. These electronic technologies are available if you look for them. JAWS converts text and components of the Windows operating system into synthesized speech. Speakup allows users to interact with applications and the GNUL/Linux operating system. VoiceOver is used in the Mac operating system. Window-Eyes is used with the Windows operating system. The American Foundation for the Blind has more information on these software and related hardware products.

Braille is a system using an arrangement of raised dots representing letters and numbers. You often see Braille in elevators and on restroom signs. Many books have been published in Braille for those who are blind or visually impaired. I understand that Unified English Braille Code (UEBC) is an English-language standard code Braille for a wide variety of literary and technical material. Nemeth Code Braille is useful in mathematics and science notation. Braille sheet music and other Braille styles are available as well. I personally have not taken the time to learn Braille, but it certainly is an option for you.

Feline Friends: I have two cats at home: a ten-year-old dense black-and-white cat named Oreo and a twenty-month-old feral cat named Lucky. Lucky is not a pancake because my wife rescued him from the middle of the road one dark night. I fed him with a little bottle for three weeks before he could lap milk. I am sure that a blind man bottle-feeding a kitten with milk splattering all over is a funny sight. Lucky is a wildly playful, young guy who likes to tease me. He is beautiful with long gray-and-smoke-colored hair and a fox-like tail. When he is fully grown, Lucky will probably become a thirteen-pound cat. One unique characteristic is that Lucky has no voice. The most he can say is "Eh." Even if you accidently step on him, the response is a quiet "Eh."

Picture this. I make a sandwich, take it to the table, and sit down to eat. When I try to take a bite of my sandwich, I bump heads with a cat. Oreo is on the other side, taking a bite as well, trying to pull the sandwich from my hand. She knows I can't see her, and she takes advantage.

Now Lucky, on the other hand, is just a thief. When I am cutting up string beans to cook, this cat quietly jumps up on the counter and steals a string bean. He does not eat the string bean. He just steals it for sport. When no one else is around, Lucky also has been known to steal bacon or kielbasa off my plate. He jumps up to the table or counter so quietly that I don't know he's there. I know Lucky has stolen something only when I hear a thump when he jumps down. Of course, Lucky does not take advantage of me when my wife, Alexis, is around because she would discipline him and chase him off the table or counter.

Martial Arts: One thing that really became apparent when I lost my eyesight is how much vision plays a part in balance. Without sight, I became clumsy and unstable. I am sure that the balance situation added to my depression. This was upsetting because I had been quite athletic. I could bicycle more than fifty miles in a day and felt strong on my feet. I even hiked up Cannon Mountain in New Hampshire, a 2,100-foot elevation change. Now I see nothing and have poor balance.

In 2015, when I became more emotionally stable, my dear friend John took me to his dojang, a formal training place for martial arts. At Mark Cashatt's Taekwon-Do School in Souderton, Pennsylvania, I met Master Mark, who consented to teach me in the system of Tai Chi, even though he had never taught a blind man before. Master Mark stated he was "up for the challenge."

The form of Tai Chi that Master Mark taught me is called Chen 18. Each of the eighteen movements in this short form required Master Mark to position me and physically guide me through the movement into the correct position or posture. He would instruct me in three different movements at a session, which I would then practice at home. Each lesson consisted of Master Mark critiquing me on the three movements learned in the prior session and then adding three more. It took me more than three months to learn all the movements of Chen 18. Then my job was to perfect my Chen 18 form, gain a smooth transition from movement to movement, maintain my balance, and become stronger.

Tai Chi movements each have a name, such as "Buddha's Warrior Attendant Pounds the Mortar," "Single Whip," or "White Crane Spreads Its Wings." Each movement can be somewhat complex and requires slow, coordinated movement of your arms and hands, positioning and movement of your feet, and distribution of weight and breathing, all with balance.

After two years of lessons and practice, I did

a solo demonstration of Chen 18 at a banquet on World Tai Chi Day, April 30, 2016. I got a standing ovation, according to my wife. However, without sight, I just need to take my wife's word.

Master Mark is also teaching me Qigong, a system of coordinated, slow-flowing movements; deep rhythmic breathing; and calming of the mind or meditation. The Qigong movements or postures I learned have helped me open up and increase the range of motion of my shoulders. Before Qigong, I could not reach around and put my right hand on the back of my neck because my shoulders were so restricted. Now I can touch the back of my neck with ease.

Tai Chi and Qigong have helped increase my strength, coordination, range of motion, balance, and stability. They are disciplines I recommend to anyone who has lost sight or is having problems with balance.

Special appreciation and thanks go out to Master Mark for his patience and dedicated training and to my friend John for taking me to the Taekwon-Do School and coaching me with form and motion.

If martial arts is not your cup of tea, I suggest you find another discipline for exercise to keep your muscles strong, joints flexible, and balance steady. Walking is excellent exercise, and so is yoga. You can buy inexpensive one-, two-, three-, four-, five-, and ten-pound weights to tone and strengthen your upper and lower body. If you are unsure on your feet, use the weights while sitting in a chair.

Consider stationary bicycles or recumbent bikes because they are safer than treadmills for blind folks and are useful to keep your legs strong while you are doing a cardio workout. If you like, join a gym or YMCA to use the equipment or pool. In other words, move your body to maintain your health and balance.

In the past, I have enjoyed bicycling and could ride long distances. Now this is just not easy. The Pennsylvania Center for Adaptive Sports in Philadelphia offers activities, where an active or athletic person works with individuals who have a disability in order to help them succeed in a sport. I am strengthening my legs again and hope that, in the near future, I will be able to ride a tandem bicycle with someone from Adaptive Sports.

Navigating: Having gone blind later on in life, I was fortunate to have had the experience of living in and getting to know the same house for more than twenty-five years. The arrangement of furniture and structure is familiar to me. Going from place A to place B within the house usually is no problem. If, for some reason, I stop or get distracted and lose my concentration, I am lost. When I lose my focus, a slight turn will bump me into the refrigerator, wall, cabinet, door frame, furniture, or whatever. At this point, after a few four-letter words, I need to put out my hands to feel for a familiar piece of furniture, wall, or doorway to reestablish the path to my destination. I have lost my way and banged my head so many times that I seem to always have a bump on my head or some scratch or abrasion. I anticipate that, by the year 2020, I will have lost all my brain cells from banging my head. (Just kidding.)

The Bureau of Blindness and Visual Services in Philadelphia helped me get a white cane to feel the area in front of me. The cane gives me insight into transitions so I am less likely to trip on something unexpected. It helps me identify hazards. I can feel a lifted sidewalk caused by a tree root, the depth of a curb or steps, and more. A white cane is essential for the mobility of a person with limited or no vision.

Kent navigating in the neighborhood.

The Bureau of Blindness and Visual Services also provided me with mobility training outside of the house. Tara took me to Montgomery Mall and coached me in the use of escalators and steps. With her, I learned how to recognize handicap ramps.

This brings up a point. Sidewalk handicap ramps are inconsistent. Some point parallel and perpendicular to the road, and others point diagonally to the middle of the intersection. Some ramps are at the corner; others are back from the corner. How is a blind person to know? Tara taught me to search the curb to orient myself so as to continue in the correct path.

As I mentioned earlier, walking in a straight line is not my forte. I find it easy to make a forty-five-degree turn instead of a ninety-degree turn, resulting in getting off course. When turning around, I might turn 160 or 200 degrees instead of 180 degrees, setting me slightly off course. My biggest problem is trying to cross a street without the orienting reference from the sound of a passing car on the street. Roads in my area are not all parallel and perpendicular.

They bend around. When I am walking, a slight bend may be undetectable, resulting in a loss of orientation and loss of my sense of direction. Navigating requires intense concentration.

When it comes to getting into a car, it is better if I open the door myself. This way I have reference to the door, its hinge, the seat, and the door frame, making it easier to sit in the seat. If someone else opens the door wide, it's much harder to orient myself and understand how to get in.

Navigating in a public restroom is a challenge. Fortunately, when needed, I have been able to ask a considerate man for guidance.

Crowded elevators create a challenge for a blind person. You need to get through the open door, walk into the elevator without bumping into people, turn around, and then keep your balance as the elevator moves.

When I walk into a crowded elevator, I usually put my hands up and say, "I am blind, and I can legally grope."

This comment usually gets a big laugh, and folks give me more room.

One time a woman replied, "You may be blind, but you can still get slapped."

Blind Chef: When it comes to cooking, my motto has always been, "If I like to eat good food, I should know how to cook good food." Over my lifetime, I have cooked many meals from simple ingredients to create delicious dishes. I used fresh vegetables, good quality meats, coconut oil, olive oil, butter, lots of seasonings, and more. However, I did not learn to bake, so I delegated breads and cakes to others.

I have worked in my kitchen for many years, and I am quite familiar with its organization. If things are not where I expect them, I become frustrated. My wife says, "If you move something, you will hear a lot of four-letter words come out of Kent."

I have always loved to cook. I have found that, even without sight, things I did in the past with repetition, I can still do now. I can still do most tasks and prepare most foods, including chopping vegetables, cooking omelets, making a stew, grilling a steak or burger, putting together a salad, or making soup from scratch.

One morning I was having difficulty getting a frying pan oriented properly on the stove. When I finally got my act together, I was able to prepare my breakfast of turkey sausage, sunny-side eggs, and multicolored potatoes. I even perfectly plated the breakfast myself. When my wife came downstairs from her shower, she took a picture of my breakfast.

Kent cooked and plated a perfect breakfast of sausage, eggs, and potatoes.

One thing to help with temperature settings on an electric stove, toaster oven, or microwave is to use puff paint or tactile dots (Bump-Dots) to mark dial locations for low, medium, high, off, or whatever you find important. The puff paint expands so you can feel its location. Bump-Dots are round, raised dots with a sticky back for easy application. Puff paint and Bump-Dots are also helpful for marking other appliances such as the clothes washer and dryer.

We have an electric stove with the old-style, exposed coils. First, I make sure nothing is on the stove that could burn—no dishes, no towels, no paper, or no plastic articles. If I am steaming vegetables, I put the water in the pot and vegetables in the steamer portion. If I am cooking an egg or frying up a burger, I put a little coconut or olive oil in the pan first. Then I center my pot or pan on one of the cold burners using my hands for guidance. I make sure the pan handle is set toward the side of the stove so it is not over a burner and it is easy to locate. I also make sure the pan handle is not facing the front of the stove so I cannot bump into it and knock the pan off the burner. When I am ready to proceed, I turn on the burner to preheat the pan. So how do I know when the food is done? I touch the meat or the egg with my finger to check the firmness.

Oh, I also barbeque using our propane infrared grill, which has three burners. Because there is no flame shooting above the metal grill, the infrared grill is much safer for me to use. I turn two burners on high and let them heat up. I set my London broil or burgers right on the grill. When I think the meat is done, I gently touch it with my finger to test for resistance and can get an idea if it is ready.

To roast beef, chicken, fish, or vegetables, I use a roasting pan and turn the left and middle burners on high to preheat. When they are up to temperature, I turn the middle burner to low and put the roasting pan on the right side over the unlit third burner. When I close the grill cover, the system operates just like an oven.

When making a cucumber salad, I use the same technique as a sighted person. I hold the cucumber on the cutting board with bent fingers of my left hand and use these fingers as a guide for the knife blade, which is in my right hand. After the cut is made, I move my left hand down the cucumber a tiny bit and cut again. Once you know this technique, you don't need to look at your work. If you watch cooking shows, the chef usually is talking and looking at the camera when slicing vegetables and not always looking at the knife.

Even though I can cook fairly well, serving can be a challenge. When I try to put the cooked food onto a plate, I often miss the plate and drop the food onto the counter or floor. To prevent a problem, I usually ask Alexis for help with the serving part.

I try to clean up after cooking, but I am not efficient at this chore. My wife kindly cleans up the mess or disaster I leave behind. And she usually doesn't tell me how bad the spills are.

Some of my delicious dishes include vegetable omelets with mushrooms, green pepper, onion, and Swiss chard with potatoes on the side. I grill a tasty London broil and serve the steak with baked sweet potatoes. I steam broccoli, collard greens, string beans, asparagus, or Brussels sprouts, adding butter or coconut oil as desired.

My wife enjoys my steamed red beets. In the summer and fall, a tomato salad with fresh basil, parsley, hemp seed, and apple cider vinegar is scrumptious. Thinly sliced cucumber, parsley, and onion tossed with a dressing of apple cider vinegar and honey is refreshing.

For poultry dishes, I use marinated or smoked turkey breasts from Bolton Market in Silverdale, Pennsylvania, because they are easy to cook, taste delicious, and are free of hormones and antibiotics. I often will put chicken legs and thighs with lots of vegetables into a pan, add tomato sauce, and simmer. Put this tomato chicken over black bean spaghetti, and there you have a gluten-free meal. Seeds of Change offers an organic quinoa and brown rice packet with garlic that I use to make a quick, one-pan meal. Add in sautéed vegetables and some beef or chicken to make the quinoa and rice mix into a wonderful dinner. Oh, I have not mentioned a meatloaf from ground beef or turkey. I put some coconut oil in the meatloaf and skip the bread crumbs. Delicious! Yes, I like to cook so that I have tasty food to eat.

Since we are talking about food, eating can be an adventure for someone who is blind. Try blindfolding yourself to experience this eating challenge.

In my cooking endeavors, I have been known to let the water evaporate out and burn a pot or two. When Alexis replaced the twenty-five-year-old Farberware pots, she was not too upset. She just cautioned me, "Please don't burn the house down." However, when I burned a brand-new stainless steel pot, my wife got very annoyed. She now buys used pots at a secondhand store and does not care if they get messed up.

When pouring liquids into a glass, I put a finger a half inch into the glass to feel the fluid level when it rises. For a carafe, coffee mug, or pitcher, you can tell when they are nearly full by the sound. My wife always knows when I make coffee. I grind fresh coffee beans and at least one whole bean gets away. It escapes onto the counter or the floor.

When it comes to plugging in the coffeepot or other appliances, I reference the round pin or grounding pin in the plug to the grounding hole in the outlet. Here in the United States the plug has two flat rectangular pieces, one with a slightly larger end. If there is no grounding round pin for reference, the wider flat piece always goes on the left side of the receptacle, provided the outlet is installed according to the standard. For plugs that have equal size flat pieces, they can be plugged in either way. Oh, you can apply Bump-Dots to the grip part of the plug or the cover plate of the outlet to mark the direction and make insertion into the outlet easier.

Mechanical Skills: More than a decade ago, I installed a shower filter to take out particles, chlorine, and other foreign chemicals from the shower water. After so many years, the shower end piece or sprayer broke. I went down to the cellar and found the old showerhead, and then came back to the bathroom and screwed in the original chrome and metal sprayer piece. It worked fine for a few months until the actual shower filter housing broke.

I can't understand why the shower filter broke after only a decade of use. The filter threads seized onto the pipe and were impossible to turn. I sprayed the fitting with WD-40 and let it sit overnight. In the morning, I found my wrench with a tightening chain and brought this tool up to the bathroom. I put the tool on the old fitting and cranked down the chain, until the filter came off, leaving the threads clean. So I installed a new filter unit, and we were ready to shower. Impressed my wife for sure!

Recently the handle for flushing the toilet broke. I purchased a new handle and rod and loosened the old nut, knowing it was a left-handed thread. I installed a new handle and rod all by feel. In addition I replaced the toilet seat to freshen up the look.

One spring, the lawn mower would not start. I went into the basement, got my plug wrench and starting fluid, and then went back outside. Just by feel, I removed the lawn mower plug, sprayed in some starting fluid, and reinstalled the plug and wire. After two pulls on the mower cord, the machine started.

Later in the summer, my neighbor also had difficulty starting her lawn mower. My wife suggested she wait until she could get Kent to help. Yes, yes, yes. I started the neighbor's lawn mower as well. Oh, I should note here that it is a good idea, especially if the mower is sputtering or stalling, to put some dry gas treatment in the fuel tank to counteract moisture that gets into the fuel.

To sharpen my lawn mower blades, I turned the Honda mower on its side with the gas fill cap toward the top to minimize fuel leakage. Do not turn the mower on its side if the gas tank is full. I disconnected the plug wire, removed the twin blades, and took them to the basement. Because I cannot see, I oriented a blade to the belt sander before I turned on the sanding unit. I put a sharp edge on each mower blade and then reinstalled the blades on the mower. Job done well!

Please stay within your mechanical skill set. If you have not worked on a lawn mower, sharpened lawn mower blades, or cooked on a stove or grill in the past, it is probably best to delegate these tasks to others so that you do not get injured. If you are familiar with these tasks, go about them safely.

Now that I have discussed many of the things I can do, let me discuss what I miss the most. I miss seeing the lovely faces and smiles of my wife, daughter, grandchildren, and friends. I miss the fun of driving my car and the excitement of driving a go-kart. I can no longer see the beautiful blue sky and wonderful flowers in my garden or see the seasons change. I miss hiking in the woods, canoeing and rafting down the Delaware River, swimming in the ocean, and bicycling with my friends. I miss visiting the museums and Historic District in Philadelphia. And most of all, I miss eye candy. What is eye candy, you wonder? Girl watching! I sure do miss my eye candy.

When I begin to feel sorry for myself, I think of blind singers, songwriters, and musicians who sold millions of records or became Grammy Award or Golden Globe winners and more. Stevie Wonder comes to mind. He sang "You Are the Sunshine of My Life" and "I Just Called to Say I Love You." I was fortunate to see Ray Charles live at Musikfest in Bethlehem, Pennsylvania. Ray Charles sang "Georgia on My Mind," Hit the Road, Jack," and "I Can't Stop Loving You." I also saw Dianne Schuur live at the Keswick Theatre in Glenside, Pennsylvania. She won Best Jazz Vocal Performance of Female in 1986 and again in 1987. And then there is Andrea Bocelli, the talented Italian tenor who brings beautiful music to the international pop, classical, and opera charts. If these blind musicians can accomplish incredible things, there is no stopping me either.

When you are blind, you can still do the things you have done before because you have the knowledge. You don't necessarily need to see to accomplish the task. So what is the purpose of all this chatter? Life does not end once you become visually impaired, blind, or hampered by another disability. Call on your prior experience and skill sets. If you use your imagination and creativity, you will be amazed at the things you can accomplish.

Chapter 7

CHARLES BONNET SYNDROME

A CCORDING TO THE Australian organization Charles Bonnet Syndrome Foundation,

Charles Bonnet syndrome (CBS) is the occurrence of phantom visions in people living with some form of eye disease who are otherwise cognitively and psychologically healthy. These phantom images co-exist with one's usual visual experience.

Vision-impaired people who experience phantom images know that what they "see" is not really there. These phantom images can include coloured blobs, geometric patterns, faces, figures, animals, flowers, buildings and even full landscapes. (Charles Bonnet Syndrome Foundation 2017)

Vision Aware of the American Foundation for the Blind describes CBS in this way,

CBS is sometimes referred to as "phantom vision" syndrome, and can be compared to "phantom limb" syndrome, in which an individual can continue to receive sensation—and even pain signals—from a limb that has been amputated. (Vision Aware 2017)

The exact cause of CBS is not really known. Several sources have made suggestions as to the cause of this strange brain phenomenon. A British organization, the Royal National Institute of Blind People, describes the cause of CBS as follows,

The main cause of CBS is loss of vision and how your brain reacts to this loss. Exactly how sight loss leads to hallucinations isn't really known, but research is slowly revealing more about how the eye and the brain work together.

Current research seems to suggest that when you are seeing real things around you, the information received from your eyes actually stops the brain from creating its own pictures. When you lose your sight, however, your brain is not receiving as much information from your eyes as it ... [once did.] Your brain can sometimes fill in these gaps by releasing new fantasy pictures, patterns or old pictures that it has stored. When this occurs, you experience these images stored in your brain as hallucinations. (Royal Institute of Blind People 2016)

My own gut feel is that since my brain is not receiving visual input, the area of my brain responsible for processing that input is bored. It needs to justify its purpose, so it throws anything it wants out there, creating its own pictures of past visual experience or made-up images.

The Royal National Institute of Blind People talks about treatment on their website,

> Currently there is no medical cure for CBS. When you experience CBS, the most effective form of treatment can come from knowing that the condition is not a mental health problem or a symptom of another disease but is due to sight loss. (Royal Institute of Blind People 2016)

A condition of visual hallucinations in those with limited or no vision is not a new phenomenon. According to Vision Aware, this condition was described more than 250 years ago,

> Charles Bonnet ... was a Swiss naturalist and philosopher and the first person to describe the syndrome.
>
> Initially, he observed symptoms of the syndrome in his 87-year-old

grandfather, who was nearly blind from cataracts, yet still "saw" men, women, birds, carriages, buildings, scaffolding, and tapestries before his eyes.

In 1760, Bonnet described his eponymous syndrome, in which he documented a range of complex visual hallucinations that occurred in seemingly psychologically intact people. (Vision Aware 2017)

My mother-in-law, Helen, was extremely visually impaired. She often complained of "horses running in front of [her]" or "treetops swaying in the wind." These annoying visual hallucinations would get her very upset. If she tried to describe them to others, they thought she was weird, crazy, and losing it mentally. Yes, she was in her eighties with some dementia, but I have no doubt that CBS caused her visual hallucinations.

When I still had true vision, even though it was very little, a checkerboard appeared in my mind's eye due to CBS. The checkerboard was always gray with one other light color: red, green, yellow, or sometimes purple. The intensity of the checkerboard faded to a light image and then came back strong. It is a continual pattern day and night, almost always present to some extent, just with varying intensities.

Initially the checkerboard was disturbing because that was all I saw. It was like looking at the same TV screen or image continually. It was unnerving. It was continuous, and I could not shut it off. Sometimes it would fade out, but never disappear. Occasionally the checkerboard interfered with sleep. I could not dim it. In a teasing way I would say, "If I had a set of checkers or chess pieces, I could play a game."

The checkerboard evolved into people sitting in a train car or station. Three people sat in the row in front of me. One person was turned sideways and resting his arm on the back of the bench. Beyond the bench was a door with an "EXIT" sign. When I had the hallucination of people on a bench, I was often riding in an automobile.

When walking with my wife or a friend,

I would sometimes see two small children walking alongside us. Other hallucinations included people alongside me who would wander into my left side, the side with an actual but nonfunctioning eye. Sometimes I would see myself at a window frame looking out at a bare tree that had lost its leaves in winter. Yet at other times I would be looking out at a landscape. Occasionally I have seen a red path with water appearing on the right. I have seen an image of vehicles, particularly pickup trucks, appear in my upper left "vision" driving to the right. I'd see all kinds of distorted images, sometimes coming toward me with animal faces. Industrial machines with fly wheels and gears would pass by. When I concentrated on an image, it would come toward me and then fade away. I have had an image of a ball coming toward me, turning into a soccer ball with writing on one of the panels, and then vanishing, only to come toward me again.

Earlier on in my journey into blindness, the images and hallucinations were very disturbing, particularly when they interrupted my sleep. I thought, *Am I going to spend the rest of my life like this?* Fortunately I learned of CBS and began to relax and accept it as something okay for me and not unusual for someone with limited or no vision.

In March 2015, I had an emergency visit to Thomas Jefferson Hospital in Philadelphia. I was having difficulty with inflammation, my joints, and walking. The Emergency Department doctor gave me an excessively high dose of the steroid prednisone and muscle relaxants. Following the high dose of the drugs, an extremely disturbing green screen appeared. It was like a bright forest. Out of the path in the woods came a marching army. The lead element of that army sometimes would be on horseback and then turn back into just men marching. After two or three days, the screen turned very bright with men on horseback holding spears moving from left to right. In the middle of the screen, toward the front, five or six people were dressed in Mongolian robes and hats. They were congregating right in front of me and moving around. This excessively bright screen and activity lasted thirty-six hours, and I couldn't sleep. It was terrible. I was exhausted. As I came down from the high dose of prednisone and got some sleep, things improved. However, this bright green screen bothered me for quite some time.

Now that I have been visually impaired for four years, it seems as though I always have some type of screen, sometimes dim or occasionally bright, but never black. The screen runs continually and randomly with varying images, movement, or color. At this time of my life, images are various forms, three-dimensional shapes, or strange or multicolored configurations, but rarely people. The images I see are random and keep morphing into something different. Sometimes I see a white screen with a red tint almost simulating daytime. If I cannot dim or turn off this image, I have trouble getting to sleep. I cannot determine a correlation between the type of pattern or image I see with what I am thinking or doing. I cannot will the image to dim or to disappear.

The times I sleep the best are when the

screen is darker, meaning less intense with indistinguishable images. I call this my "nighttime image." If I start into the night with a dull screen and I keep my mind clear, I fall asleep more easily. If not, I can lie awake most of the night. In this situation, sometimes listening to soft music or a talking book will put me to sleep.

I cannot determine a correlation between phases of the moon or CBS images and my ability to sleep. I must say that sleeping is a problem for me. Many nights I lie awake for hours, making it difficult to function normally the following day. When I get into this pattern of poor sleep and daytime fatigue, I have a hard time getting back into a normal circadian rhythm. Daytime naps just do not compensate for a poor night's sleep.

To understand CBS, think of being stuck in front of a TV in a dark room with eyelids taped up so you could only look at the TV and not close your eyelids. The screen has varying intensities with only two or three images moving around. You must look at this screen more than twenty-four continuous hours. Could you sleep? Could you think rationally? How would you feel emotionally?

All in all, I have learned to be *not bothered* by these CBS hallucinations, as long as they do not interrupt sleep. It is very weird, but something I must live with.

Chapter 8

INTERACTION WITH FAMILY AND FRIENDS

THERE IS NO doubt that after I accepted my blindness, family and friends help me maintain a positive attitude. I am fortunate that I have close family and friends who take the time to care. Their kind support helps me deal with my blindness and motivates me each day. This makes me feel that I am not alone in my journey in life and that my blindness is a hindrance, not a death sentence.

I realize that some friends or family members just don't know how to interact with me. After all, what does one say to a blind man? What does one do with a blind guy? How can one be of help? I try to reassure these folks by saying,

"Be yourself, and interact with me as always. I might just need a ride or a little guidance when walking outside the house. I am the same Kent as always. I just cannot see."

Family: I have been incredibly fortunate that my wife, Alexis, is loving and productive and sees to it that I have what I need. Alexis works full-time while managing to take care of the banking, pay the bills, do the laundry and housework, maintain the yard, and cook meals I cannot manage on my own. Alexis also tends the vegetable garden during the season.

When our two moms with dementia were alive and my eyesight was diminishing, Alexis was always busy seeing to their care. And in her spare time, she has taken me to more than 250 appointments with medical doctors, dentists, ophthalmologists, optometrists, chiropractors, acupuncturists, naturopaths, social workers, hospitals, and labs for testing. Somehow my wife fits it all into her schedule, and she rarely takes time for herself.

My wedding in Hamilton, Bermuda, on May
23, 1989. The prosthetic in the right eye does
not team perfectly with the good left eye.

As much as possible, Alexis takes me out to
do our shopping. Together we go to grocery,
department and hardware stores, as well as
greenhouses and outdoor farmers' markets.
Since I have been shopping in these stores for
many years, I have become very familiar with
them. Often Alexis will explain what she is
looking at so that I understand my options and
can decide what I want to buy.

Grocery shopping with Alexis leading the cart.

In the market, I hold the handle of the shopping cart while my wife pulls from the front. In Costco one time, my wife did not notice I let go of the cart for a second. She pulled the cart along at a fast pace, and I needed to use my white cane to slowly walk forward. As the distance increased, onlookers began to wonder. When my wife walked more than forty feet with the cart, she turned around and found me missing or unattached. In shock her response was "Oh my goodness, I lost Kent. I am sorry. I am so sorry. I lost Kent." The onlookers all burst out laughing.

To minimize my bumping into things when the store aisles are very tight, Alexis leaves me in a safe place and goes down the aisle herself to get the needed items. When I am standing by myself, I sometimes feel like a carved cigar store Indian sculpture. I guess I should hold a sign advertising something, and then maybe we would get a store discount or trinket. In any case, doing the shopping allows me to get out into the community and bring some sense of normalcy to my life. It makes me feel like a functioning member of my family and society.

My wife loves to watch my two grandsons Austin and Gavin guide me around. They are so companionate. They have learned to prevent me from bumping my head in a doorway, step safely down a curb, not trip on a raised sidewalk, and more. My daughter, Hope, sometimes takes me to the grocery store, the local Telford Farmer's Market, and my grandsons' sports games.

Kent is proud of grandson Austin
graduating from high school.

Kent with grandson Gavin.

My brother, Charles, is a special person too. I respect him, love him, and appreciate his friendship. Charles calls me regularly to stay in touch, discuss hot topics and politics, and always provide encouragement. This interaction is important to keep me grounded and feeling connected.

Friends: My life has been enriched by numerous friends and acquaintances over the years, some of whom have become very dear. For the most part, they have been able to make me feel part of the group. It is impossible in a few sentences to describe all the wonderful times and cherished moments we have shared.

Knowing I have special people in my life has had a major positive impact on my adjustment and the acceptance of my blindness. With them, I am accepted as the person I have always been. They insulate me from depression. I am so fortunate to have this core of special friends. I am so blessed that these people are part of my life.

- John has been a close and generous friend since the early 1970s. He has taken me to Tai Chi regularly and has coached me in form and movement. John has accompanied me to several doctors' appointments and makes sure my health needs are cared for. We ventured to Musikfest to hear different types of music and he has guided me around the town. John has also taken me fishing and makes sure that I don't fall out of the boat.

- Gail and Jeff invite me to many social gatherings. They always make my birthday special. They are so much fun. They have graciously given their time and energy to make me feel good. Gail and Jeff have devoted time to help out in my gardens too. Wonderful friends and love to them both.

- I have known Chad for more than two years now, and he has become a special friend, as well. Chad introduces me to books and knowledge which stimulate my mind. Chad is so generous and considerate. He takes me for long walks in the park, takes me to lunch and helps organize my CD collection. Chad telephones me at least once a week to engage in conversation and this is an encouragement to me. We always find ways to laugh together.

- Mark has been most kind with me as I learn Tai Chi and Qigong. He patiently takes me through the various movements and postures until I get it. He has been incredible in helping me to maintain my focus and balance. Much appreciation goes out to Mark.

- In our locale, several business networking groups have welcomed me, not as a business member, but as a perennial guest. My wife, who represents her massage business, takes me with her to the Networking Group of Indian Valley, (NGIV), and to the Quakertown Business Networking Group (QBNG). It has been wonderful for me to be accepted for who I am by the members and interact with these folks in the community. Thank you to all my business networking friends for your kindness.

- Neighbors have taken me to concerts, hauled the trash totes from curbside up the driveway, helped my wife with snow removal, cut some of the grass, and rescued me when I was lost. Thank you to Joe, John, Ray, Roberta and Vince.

- I want to say thank you to the health care providers who have maintained my physical, mental and emotional health: Dr. Claire, Dr. Joe, Dr. John, and Dr. Ria. These professionals have helped to take away the pain. Social workers Sue and Patty guided my mind and emotions in a positive direction.

- My new photographer friend Bruce introduced me to a poignant song written in 1975 by British songwriter John Dawson Read. The lyrics put to beautiful music make the song "A Friend of Mine Is Going Blind" emotionally moving. I Googled the song title and played the song online. The song begins with the words "A friend of mine is going blind, but through the dimness he sees so much better than me" (Read 1975). Thank you, Bruce, for pointing me to this heart-warming song.

- Special thanks and appreciation go out to all those at the Bucks County Association for the Blind and Visually Impaired: Ellen, Gaye, Sheryl, John, Larry, JP, and other support staff. These folks have given me the opportunity to interact with others in my situation, taught me about living with my disability, and guided me in obtaining the technology to keep me in touch with the world around me. Appreciation goes out to Donna and Megan for their meeting confirmation calls.

Bucks County Association for the
Blind and Visually Impaired picking
up Kent for a group meeting.

- Thanks to Tara at the Bureau of Blindness and Visual Services for all her mobility training and friendship. She made sure I know how to use the white cane, how to find my way on sidewalks, and how to use an escalator. We always had great discussions, too.
- Special thanks to the Carnegie Library of Pittsburgh for all the talking books they have shared with me. I look forward

to getting the mail each day to see what new books they have sent. The Library for the Blind and Physically Handicapped of the Free Library of Philadelphia keeps me knowledgeable of current events through regular periodicals on disk. This organization deserves kudos, as well.

All my love and appreciation goes out to friends and family members. Without these wonderful folks in my life, it would have been extremely difficult to adjust to a new life style with no sight. They gave me the strength and guidance to persevere and grow. I am grateful to each one of you for being an integral part of my journey. Thank you to all.

Chapter 9

CLOSING REMARKS

I HOPE THAT you have gained useful information through sharing my experiences and insights in this book and enjoyed a few laughs along the way. It has been a long and difficult road since 2009 when my eyesight began to fail. Somehow I worked through the physical and emotional challenges, sometimes with help from family, friends, and health-related professionals. You can work through your challenges as well. You can get through the many ups and downs, move forward, and get back to the business of living your life.

Here are some of the thoughts that I hope you take away. My wish is that you find your journey easier through knowing my experiences.

- Keep in mind that blindness and other disabilities are a hindrance not a death sentence.

- Knowing my story of emotional ups and downs and emergence into a state of acceptance will help you through your own journey in life.

- Call on your experience and skill sets along with imagination and creativity. You will be amazed at the things you can accomplish.

- Please take from my experience and techniques to add to your skill set to use in your everyday activities.

- Check out professionals and organizations that can be of help to you in your personal journey. Contacts for some of these are in the Appendix.

- I hope I have whet your appetite for the advantageous use of modern-day technology such as iPhone, web browsers, Be My Eyes, Adobe Digital Editor, JAWS Screen Reader, other software, optical character readers, and more.

- Maybe a service dog is right for your situation. A dog just did not work out for me.
- Never underestimate the value of humor to get you through.
- Move your body to keep you healthy and to maintain your emotional and physical balance.
- Refer to a quote from the book *Yes I Can ... Yes I Will ...* by Dr. Ria M. Gilday, "Opportunity is a choice you make, not a social obligation."

I wish you well on your own journey through life.

Appendix

ORGANIZATIONS THAT CAN HELP

MANY ORGANIZATIONS ARE dedicated to helping folks with disabilities and provide products and services designed to assist them. Web browsers for the Internet are useful to help find these organizations and provide contact information.

Some of the organizations listed below have been of help to me. The contact information was accurate July 1, 2017 but may change in the future.

Websites Providing Information and Contacts

American Foundation for the Blind

Website: www.afb.org/directory.
aspx?action=results
Services: Large number of contacts
categorized by state

Vision Aware

Joint program of the American Foundation
for the Blind and Reader's Digest Partners for
Sight Foundation
Website: www.VisionAware.org
E-mail: visionaware@afb.net
Services: Information on eye conditions
and support services

Organizations That Have Been of Help to Me

American Brain Tumor Association

8550 W. Bryn Mawr Avenue, Suite 550
Chicago, IL 60631
Phone: 773.577.8750 and 800.886.2282
Fax: 773.577.8738
E-mail: info@abta.org

Website: www.abta.org

American Foundation for the Blind

AFB Headquarters

2 Penn Plaza, Suite 1102

New York, NY 10121

Phone: 212.502.7600 / General information:
    800.232.5463 (800 AFB-LINE)

Fax: 888.545.8331

Website: www.afb.org

Website: www.afb.org/store (to order a
    print or online publication or download
    a publication catalog)

Services: Information on products for
    people who are blind or visually
    impaired

AccessWorld®

Services: AFB's monthly online technology
    magazine with reviews of technology
    products and online resources for
    people with vision loss

Associated Services for the Blind & Visually Impaired

919 Walnut Street

Philadelphia, PA 19107

Phone: 215.627.0600

Fax: 215.922.0692

Website: www.asb.org

Bucks County Association for the Blind and Visually Impaired (BCABVI)

400 Freedom Drive

Newtown, PA 18940

Phone: 215.968.9400 and 800.472.8775

E-mail: info@bucksblind.org

Website: www.bucksblind.org

Bureau of Blindness and Visual Services (BBVS)

444 North 3rd Street – 5th floor

Philadelphia, PA 19123

Phone: 215.560.5700

Website: www.pcacares.
org/service_provider/
bureau-of-blindness-visual-services
Philadelphia Corporation for Aging, Office
of Vocational Rehabilitation

Charles Bonnet Syndrome Foundation

PO Box 352, Flinders Lane

VIC, 8009.

Australia

Website: www.charlesbonnetsyndrome.org

Enhanced Vision

5882 Machine Drive

Huntington Beach, CA 92649

Phone: 888.811.3161

Website: www.enhancedvision.com/low-vision-product-line.html

Website: www.enhancedvision.com/low-vision-resources/pennsylvania-low-vision-resources.html

Services: Low-vision products and information

Independent Living Aids, LLC

137 Rano Road

Buffalo, NY 14207

Phone: 800.537.2118 and 855.746.7452

Fax: 855.937.3906

Website: www.independentliving.com

Library for the Blind and Physically Handicapped (LBPH), Carnegie Library of Pittsburgh

4724 Baum Boulevard

Pittsburgh, PA 15213

Phone: 412.687.2440 and 800.242.0586

Website: www.carnegielibrary.org/
clp_location/library-for-the-blind-and-
physically-handicapped

Services: A network library of the Library of
Congress

Library for the Blind and Physically Handicapped (LBPH) of the Free Library of Philadelphia

919 Walnut Street

Philadelphia, PA 19107

Phone: 215.683.3213

Website: www.freelibrary.org

Lighthouse Guild

250 West 64th Street

New York, NY 10023

Phone: 800.284.4422

Website: www.lighthouseguild.org

Lions Center for the Blind

Oakland, CA center closing August, 2017

Phone: 510.450.1580

Website: www.lbcenter.org

MaxiAids

42 Executive Blvd.

Framingdale, NY 11735

Phone: Sales 800.522.6294 / Customer
    Support 631.752.0521

Fax: 631.752.0689

Website: www.maxiaids.com

Services: Products for blind and low vision

Montgomery County Association for the Blind (MCAB)

25 E. Marshall Street, 3rd floor

Norristown, PA 19401

Phone: 215.661.9800

Fax: 610.292.7191

Website: www.mcab.org

National Federation of the Blind of Pennsylvania

1500 Walnut Street, Suite 200

Philadelphia, Pennsylvania 19102

Phone: NFB of PA: 215.988.0888

E-mail: president@nfbp.org

Website: www.nfbp.org

National Library Service for the Blind and Physically Handicapped, Library of Congress

Website: www.loc.gov/nls

Services: A national network of cooperating libraries providing a library program of Braille and audio materials, along with music appreciation, history, and instruction materials that all may read

Pennsylvania Center for Adaptive Sports

4 Boat House Row

Philadelphia, PA 19130

Phone: 215.765.5118 and 215.765.5119

Email: pcas@centeronline.com

Website: www.centeronline.com

National Center on Health, Physical Activity and Disability (NCHPAD)

Bucks County Transport, Inc.

PO Box 510

Holicong, PA 18928

Phone: General information: 215.794.5554

Phone: Reservations: 888.795.0740

Website: www.bctransport.org

Services: Senior Citizen Shared Ride
Program, Medical Assistance
Transportation Program, and Persons
with Disabilities Transportation
Program

Suburban Transit Network, Inc. known as
TransNet

980 Harvest Drive, Suite 100

Blue Bell, PA 19442

Phone: 215.542.7433

Fax: 215.542.8877

E-mail: ride@suburbantransit.org

Website: www.suburbantransit.org

Services: Disability services, medical
assistance, and Share Rides (for
seniors)

WORKS CITED

American Brain Tumor Association. 2014. "Meningioma." American Brain Tumor Association. Accessed April 1, 2017. www. abta.org/brain-tumor-information/types-of-tumors/meningioma.html.

Braves.com. 2017. "The Hammer." MLB Advanced Media, LP. Accessed April 3. Atlanta.braves. mlb.com/atl/history/aaron.jsp.

Cardinals.com. 2017. "Stan Musial 1920–2013." MLB Advanced Media LP. Accessed April 3. stlouis.cardinals.mlb.com/stl/fan_forum/ stan_musial.jsp?loc=achievements.

Charles Bonnet Syndrome Foundation. 2017. "Charles Bonnet Syndrome: The Condition." Charles Bonnet Syndrome Foundation. Accessed April 1. www.

charlesbonnetsyndrome.org/index.php/cbs/ the-condition.

Demmitt, Audrey. 2015. "My Review of the Be My Eyes App." Center for the Visually Impaired. Accessed April 8, 2017. www.cviga.org/sightseeing/ safe_sight_review_of_be_my_eyes_app.

Gilday, Dr. Ria M. 2000. *Yes I Can ... Yes I Will ...* RGE, Inc.

Kübler-Ross, Elizabeth. 1969. *On Death and Dying.* New York: Scribner.

Malcolm, Tim. 2009. "100 Greatest Phillies: 6—Richie Ashburn." Phillies Nation. Accessed April 1, 2017. www.philliesnation. com/2009/03/100-greatest-phillies-6-richie- ashburn.

NLS Factsheets. 2015. "Music Services for Individuals Who Are Blind or Have a Physical Disability." Library of Congress. Accessed April 1, 2017. www.loc.gov/nls/reference/ guides/music.html.

NLS: That All May Read. 2015. "Bureau of Engraving and Printing U.S. Currency Reader Program." Library of Congress.

Accessed April 1, 2017. www.loc.gov/nls/
other/currencyreader/index.html.

Read, John Dawson. 1975. "A Friend of Mine Is
Going Blind." John Dawson Read. Accessed
April 1, 2017. www.johndawsonread.com/
friend.php.

Redsox.com. 2017. "Ted Williams." MLB
Advanced Media LLP. Accessed April 3.
Boston.redsox.mlb.com/bos/history/
bos_history_williams.jsp.

Royal Institute of Blind People. 2016.
"Understanding Charles Bonnet Syndrome."
Royal Institute of Blind People. Accessed
April 1, 2017. www.rnib.org.uk/eye-health-
your-guide-charles-bonnet-syndrome-cbs/
understanding-charles-bonnet-syndrome.

That All May Read …. 2017. "National Library
Service for the Blind and Physically
Handicapped (NLS)." Library of Congress.
Accessed April 1, 2017. www.loc.gov/nls/
index.html.

Vision Aware. 2017. "Charles Bonnet
Syndrome: Why Am I Having These Visual
Hallucinations?" Vision Aware. Accessed

April 1. www.visionaware.org/info/your-eye-condition/guide-to-eye-conditions/charles-bonnet-syndrome/125.

Vision Therapy Center. 2017. "Research Overlooks Impact of Vision Problems on Motion Sickness." The Vision Therapy Center, Inc. Accessed April 1, 2017. www.thevisiontherapycenter.com/discovering-vision-therapy/research-overlooks-impact-of-vision-problems-on-motion-sickness.

Printed in the United States
By Bookmasters